The
See-Saw Tree

Book, music and lyrics by
David Wood

Samuel French – London
New York – Sydney – Toronto – Hollywood

THE SEE-SAW TREE

The See-Saw Tree was originally commissioned by the Redgrave Theatre, Farnham. The first performance was given by the Farnham Repertory Company, sponsored by Arundell House Securities, on 18th March 1986, with the following cast:

Mrs Wise/Owl	Patricia Samuels
Mrs Dunnock/Dunnock	Alex Kingston
Mr Storer/Squirrel	Christopher Reeks
Mr Jay/Jay	Kit Thacker
Mr Batty/Bat	Paul Benzing
Mrs Thrush/Mistlethrush	Brenda Longman
Mrs Cook/Cuckoo	Sharon Courtney
Mr Bunn/Rabbit	Andrew Sargent

Director: **Stephen Barry and Kit Thacker**
Production Designer: **Juliet Shillingford**
Lighting Designer: **Vincent Herbert**
Wardrobe: **Sue Cowley**
Sound: **Ghee Bowman**
Stage Management: **Fiona Francombe**
Musical Direction: **Peter Pontzen**

The See-Saw Tree was subsequently presented at Sadler's Wells Theatre, London, and on tour by Whirligig Theatre in the autumn of 1987, with the following cast:

Mrs Wise/Owl	Susannah Bray
Mrs Dunnock/Dunnock	Mary Ann Coburn
Mr Storer/Squirrel	Mike Elles
Mr Jay/Jay	Richard Hague
Mr Batty/Bat	Michael Seraphim
Mrs Thrush/Mistlethrush	Caroline High
Mrs Cook/Cuckoo	Shelaagh Ferrell
Mr Bunn/Rabbit	David Bale

Director: **David Wood**
Set & Costumes designed by **Susie Caulcutt**
Musical Supervisor: **Peter Pontzen**
Musical Director: **Michael Haslam**
Lighting by **Roger Frith**
Sound by **Paul Farrah**

**For Common Ground, the conservation
group who sowed the seed**

& THE GREEN MAN ·

TREES, WOODS

COMMON GROUND

IMAGE BY BEN NICHOLSON

I wish to acknowledge with gratitude the helpful advice given me by
Jim Flegg, whose excellent book *Oakwatch* (published by Pelham
Books) confirmed my belief that here was subject matter for a play,
and encouraged me to proceed. The subsequent use of Jim Flegg as a
sounding-board for ideas and as an oracle of the oak has been not only
extremely useful but also most enjoyable. Thank you, Jim!

D.W.

INTRODUCTION

Trees are such potent symbols to children: the climbing tree—a challenge and a friendly home, a place to dream dreams in and to make ambushes from; the Christmas tree—embodying the security and closeness of family life, the excitement of what gifts it might hold for us . . .

Trees are a measure of our own lifespans, tangible yardsticks against which we can gauge our own passing years. And when they die suddenly, or are felled, we feel their loss as if a part of us, or an old friend, had gone:

> Woodman, spare that tree!
> Touch not a single bough!
> In youth it sheltered me,
> And I'll protect it now.

But do we, as G. P. Morris suggests we should in the poem quoted above, protect them now, in adulthood? The reverse is nearer the truth. Half of the ancient woodlands that existed in 1945 have now been cut down to make way for fields of wheat and barley and regiments of taxman-friendly plantations of alien conifers. We have fewer trees in England than any other country in Europe, except Ireland.

Nearer to our own homes we are just as cavalier. Almost half of the ten million trees planted in Britain each year die through lack of care; and one of the favourite occupations of people who have just moved house is to cut down the mature trees in their newly acquired gardens.

Our ambivalence towards trees is curious since they have so much to offer us: their timber for furniture, buildings and fuel; their oxygen, their shade and compost; their beauty and the stories they could tell us if we had the imagination to hear them; and the wealth of wildlife they support.

Ancient woodlands (woodlands which are known to have existed in the Middle Ages and where there has been a continuous history of woodland cover to the present day) are the richest of our wildlife habitats, owing to their age and to the continuity of their sympathetic management. More species of birds are associated with woodlands than with any other habitat type and nearly half of the British butterflies and moths are found there. Ancient woodlands are also rich in plants: about 240 species, including about 20 different ferns, are directly associated with woodlands and, of these, 76 are entirely confined to them.

Single old trees (such as the See-Saw Tree featured in this play) are one of the most important features in town and country. They are beautiful to look at, they provide habitats and food for countless animals and birds—an old oak tree can support nearly 300 different insects and over 300 lichens—and they are landmarks which provide continuity with the past.

When *Common Ground* was preparing its project on "Trees, Woods and the Green Man", we debated on how best the project could have an impact and how we could play our part in conserving our heritage of trees and woods. Our conclusion was that our cultural relationship with trees has been aired less well than our ecological need for them, and that the ecological argument alone is not saving enough trees or fostering a widespread caring attitude to them.

What *Common Ground* hopes to contribute is a redressing of the balance by concentrating on the cultural lineage of our relationship with trees, in the past and now. We are overtly encouraging people in the arts to celebrate trees and woods through their work, and so producing an enduring legacy of books, exhibitions, plays and festivals for present and future generations to call on and to act as compelling reminders.

David Wood's play *The See-Saw Tree* was the first manifestation of the "Trees, Woods and the Green Man" project. Commissioned by the Redgrave Theatre, Farnham, it had its first performance in March 1986. The issues the play raises are ones which will confront us all at some time and we hope that it will give us the courage to make the right choices and to defend our local tree or wood when the time comes. In the words of the English poet A. E. Housman:

> Give me a land of boughs in leaf,
> A land of trees that stand;
> Where trees are fallen there is grief,
> I love no leafless land.

Angela King
Common Ground, 1987

Note

Common Ground was established in 1983 to promote the importance of our common cultural heritage—common plants and animals, familiar and local places, local distinctiveness and our links with the past, and to explore the emotional value these things have for us by forging practical and philosophical links between the arts and the conservation of nature, landscape and place.

In a Nutshell—a manifesto for trees and a guide to growing and protecting them, by Neil Sinden for *Common Ground*, and

Holding Your Ground—an action guide to local conservation (Wildwood House 1987) are both available in bookshops and from *Common Ground*, 45 Shelton Street, London WC2H 9HJ.

PRODUCTION NOTES

CHARACTERS
Each actor plays two parts, the human role linked with the animal role.

ACTOR 1: **Mrs Wise**—the Chairperson of the Parish Council. Solid, fair and authoritative.
Owl—the leader of the oak community.

ACTOR 2: **Mrs Dunnock**—Secretary of the Parish Council. Keeps a low profile. Efficient, helpful, knowledgeable, but unshowy.
Dunnock—a rather drab, hardworking bird, willing to perform menial tree tasks, cleaning, taking messages, etc.

ACTOR 3: **Mr Storer**—business-like, financially orientated Treasurer of the Parish Council.
Squirrel—home-loving, conservative, occasionally excitable member of the tree community.

ACTOR 4: **Mr Jay**—rather flashy supermarket owner, smarmy business man, ingratiating.
Jay—a flash itinerant member of the tree community, popping in and out almost as a travelling salesman, on the look-out for a good opportunity.

ACTOR 5: **Mrs Thrush**—a fairly outspoken woman, who takes public service seriously and loudly espouses a cause.
Mistlethrush—a strident member of the tree community, builder of untidy nests, not afraid to be outspoken.

ACTOR 6: **Mrs Cook**—not a local person, but not afraid to put her views. Might be regarded as somewhat common by the residents.
Cuckoo—an itinerant visitor to the tree, a colourful character from Africa, whose sole motive for visiting is to dump her egg in some unsuspecting bird's nest.

ACTOR 7: **Mr Bunn**—a concerned conservationist. Outspoken.
Rabbit—a member of the animals' underground movement. Resistance leader. Practical.

ACTOR 8:   **Mr Batty**—entrepreneur, whizz-kid smooth operator.
           Bat—hi-tech way-out member of the tree community. His
           radar comes in useful. He has big headphones connected to a
           "Walkman" style radio.

SET AND COSTUMES
The play takes place in three locations.

1) A Village Hall. This could be represented by nothing more than a table
and chairs, against tabs or plain backing.

2) The Bottom of an Oak Tree—i.e. the base of the trunk. The scale will be
quite large—bearing in mind that the characters in the play live on the tree.
Various knobs and root-formations sprout from the bottom, which might
be used as "seats". If possible, the entrance to **Rabbit**'s burrow should be
incorporated. Ivy climbing the tree could afford masking for scaffolding or
ladder-like rungs, down which and up which characters can climb.

3) Further up the Oak Tree. This will be the basic set, on which most of the
play takes place. It will hopefully include various levels, dominated by, at
stage level, the "hollow"—the home of **Owl**. This should incorporate a
closed-off section, which could be like a hut, complete with door; however, it
might be more appropriate, and less fantasy-orientated, to have a portion
partitioned off by a leafy equivalent of a bead curtain. **Owl**'s hollow
becomes the main acting area, at which meetings of the tree community take
place. Other important locations are a hole in the trunk in which **Squirrel**
has his drey, an upper level for **Mistlethrush**'s nest, and a branch from which
Bat can "hang". (N.B.: for practical reasons, it is not necessary for the actor
to hang by his legs, as it were! As long as he can support himself on his arms,
with his legs in the air, and his head thus pointing downwards, the illusion
should be acceptable.) Branches should provide walkways between the
locations, or the set could be stylized, using scaffolding and steps. However,
the set should certainly bear a token resemblance to an oak tree, and the use
of levels is important when seeing the characters visit one another.
   The costumes need not be realistic in any way. There will not be very
much time for the actors to change from their human roles to their animal
roles. Maybe half-masks could be of use, or basic identification factors. In
other words, we should not be disguising the fact that actors, indeed the
human characters in the play, are playing the parts of the tree inhabitants.

"SAVE OUR TREE"

L to R: JAY Richard Hague, **SQUIRREL** Mike Elles, **OWL** Susannah Bray, **RABBIT** David Bale, **BAT** Michael Seraphim, **CUCKOO** Shelaagh Ferrell, **MISTLETHRUSH** Caroline High, **DUNNOCK** Mary Ann Coburn

THE COMPANY WITH THE SEE-SAW TREE

Jay How's about some fresh mistletoe berries, Mistlethrush?

L to R: **DUNNOCK** Mary Ann Coburn, **MISTLETHRUSH** Caroline High, **Jay**
Richard Hague

Rabbit I tried. I did try. There was nothing I could do. Murderers! Murderers!
L to R: **RABBIT** David Bale, **SQUIRREL** Mike Elles, **OWL** Susannah Bray

THE PUBLIC MEETING

L to R: **MR BATTY** Michael Seraphim, **MR JAY** Richard Hague, **MR STORER** Mike Elles, **MISS WISE** Susannah Bray, **MRS DUNNOCK** Mary Ann Coburn

RABBIT BITES THE CABLE

L to R: SQUIRREL Mike Elles, OWL Susannah Bray, BAT Michael Seraphim, CUCKOO Shelaagh Ferrell, MISTLETHRUSH Caroline High, DUNNOCK Mary Ann Coburn, RABBIT David Bale

ACT I

As the audience arrives, the stage resembles a public platform with table and chairs

Music 1

Mrs Dunnock, a few minutes before "curtain up", sweeps the platform

Mrs Wise, the Chairperson, arrives and bids "Good-day" to Mrs Dunnock, then settles herself in the chair

Mr Jay and Mr Storer also arrive, greet each other and Mrs Wise, then sit down. Mr Jay prepares some maps and pictures

In the auditorium, Mr Batty, Mrs Thrush, Mrs Cook and Mr Bunn sit amongst the audience, near the front

When the play is due to start, Mrs Dunnock rings a small bell, and takes her seat at the table, as Secretary, taking notes. The House Lights stay up

Mrs Wise Welcome, everybody, to this public meeting. Thank you for taking the trouble to come along to discuss the future of Turner's Field, the patch of waste land next to Jay's Supermarket. As Chairperson of the Parish Council, I invite you to make your views known. Mrs Dunnock, our Secretary, will make notes on the proceedings.

Mrs Dunnock (*shyly*) Thank you, Mrs Wise. (*Correcting herself*) Madam Chairman.

Mrs Wise First, the Treasurer, Mr Storer, will outline our proposals.

Mr Storer Thank you, Madam Chairman. As you may know, Turner's Field was left in his will to the Council by Farmer Turner, who died last year. For a long time it has been unused—except as an unofficial unsightly rubbish tip—and we feel the time has come to decide its future. We are pleased that Mr Jay, here——

Mr Jay (*smiling broadly, almost smarmily*) Good afternoon.

Mr Storer —the owner of the supermarket, has offered a substantial sum for the land, and, let's face it, the Council desperately needs the cash to help improve local services ...

Mrs Thrush (*from the floor, standing*) Hear, hear. They could do with it. Our road's in a shocking state. Like driving on cobblestones ...

Mr Storer Yes, indeed. So, Mr Jay, please reveal your plans.

Mr Jay (*rising*) Certainly Mr Storer. As you know, Jay's Supermarket aims to provide a service. High quality, low prices, that's our motto. For some time, in our quest to make shopping a happy, *family* experience, we have improved our facilities—more tills for speedier checkouts, easy-push trolleys, music to soothe the harassed housewife. And now, in our usual caring way, we propose to create, (*showing a map*) on Turner's Field . . . guess what?

Mrs Cook (*from the floor, standing*) More car parking space. That's what's needed. I'm not a local, but I come here to shop and it's always a dreadful problem finding a space, then humping the shopping to the car . . .

Mr Jay Maybe, Mrs er——

Mrs Cook Cook.

Mr Jay Cook. Maybe. But, may I be so bold—do you have children?

Mrs Cook Yes, but I never bring *them* here. They get bored. I leave them with a friend.

Mr Jay Exactly. They get bored. That's why we propose to create a children's playground, where our customers' children can safely play till the shopping is successfully accomplished.

Mrs Thrush I support that. There's so little for the kids to do in this place. Not even a cinema any more.

Mrs Wise Yes, well, Mrs er——

Mrs Thrush Thrush.

Mrs Wise Mrs Thrush. Thank you. Let's have a vote. Please raise your hands if you like Mr Jay's idea of a children's playground. (*She encourages the audience to raise their hands*) Fine. Thank you.

Whatever the outcome . . .

Mr Bunn (*from the floor, standing*) Madam Chairman, before I vote, could I know more of what this playground will be like? Will it be an adventure playground? Swings, slides, that type of thing?

Mrs Wise Mr Jay.

Mr Jay Ah, yes, well to answer that, may I, Madam Chairman, invite Mr Batty to speak? I will be giving Mr Batty the concession to create the playground and operate it.

Mr Bunn Concession? You mean this is a business deal?

Mr Jay Well, life's a business, Mr er——

Mr Bunn Bunn.

Mr Jay Mr Bunn. Mr Batty, please . . .

Mr Batty joins the others on the platform. He displays a diagram

Mr Batty Yes, well, like I'm going to clear the land and have an open play area with swings and slides, all free for the use of, plus a special building for the machines.

Mr Bunn Machines?

Mr Batty Yes. The space invaders, the pin tables, the fruit machines . . .

Mrs Wise And, Mr Batty, will these be er . . . free for the use of?

Mr Batty Ah. Well. No. Like I've got to make a living, Madam Chairman.

Mr Jay Seems fair enough to me. Only providing what the kids of today really want.

Mr Bunn So, Mr Batty, you are going to clear the land, are you?

Mr Batty Yes.

Mr Bunn On that land are several trees. Healthy trees.

Mr Batty Can't help that. They'll have to come down.

Mr Bunn But one of those trees is an oak. It's been there for nearly three hundred years.

Mr Batty So what?

Mr Bunn So what? (*He goes on to the platform*) That tree has a history. In the old days people called it the See-Saw Tree.

Mr Batty The See-Saw Tree?

Mr Bunn The See-Saw Tree.

Music 2

The Lighting changes. Mr Bunn remains in a pin-spot, while the rest of the stage grows dark. The actors clear the stage as Mr Bunn speaks

One of its branches grew straight out, near to the ground. Children used to balance a plank over the branch and use it as a see-saw. The villagers loved that oak. And the tree was itself like a village. A living community of animals, birds and insects, going about their daily business. It still is.

During the following speech, an actor hands Mr Bunn his "Rabbit" costume and, if necessary, helps him on with it

Just imagine what that community will feel like should it be threatened. Just imagine what might happen if Mr Jay's plan went ahead and Mr Batty was allowed to cut down that oak tree, that special oak tree. Just imagine. (*Echo effect*) Just imagine, just imagine . . .

The Lighting changes as the CURTAINS *part to reveal the base of the oak tree. The trunk is wide, bearing in mind that the characters are small. Various knob-like shapes and root formations sprout from the bottom, which might be used as "seats". The entrance to Rabbit's burrow is incorporated. Ivy climbing the tree could afford masking for scaffolding or ladder-like rungs, down which and up which characters can climb. Foliage is visible above. A few acorns lie on the ground. Grass grows around the roots. A large white cross has been painted or chalked on the trunk*

Mr Bunn "becomes" Rabbit

Music 3

It is dawn. A chorus of birdsong is heard

Rabbit chooses a likely blade of grass and begins eating it. He makes for his burrow, but suddenly sees the white cross. Mystified, he approaches it and stretches up to feel it. It is still wet. He examines the paint on his paw, then looks at the cross again

Suddenly Dunnock's head peers through the foliage above

Dunnock Morning, Rabbit.

Rabbit jumps and turns

Rabbit Oh it's you, Dunnock. Morning. You're up early.

Dunnock Lots to do, Rabbit. A Dunnock's work is never done. Owl's hollow to clean, Squirrel's drey to muck out . . .

Rabbit (*idea*) Squirrel?

Dunnock Yes, he's doing his annual acorn tally. Stock-taking. Takes it so seriously . . .

Rabbit Dunnock, give him a message will you? It's urgent.

Dunnock S'pose so. If he's in.

Rabbit Please. There's a mystery to solve.

Dunnock How exciting. The only mystery I've got to solve is how I'm going to get all my jobs done. You've no idea how——

Rabbit Go. Now. Tell Squirrel to meet me here. As soon as possible.

Dunnock All right, all right. Keep your fur on. (*Disappearing*) Dear oh dear oh dear.

Dunnock exits

Rabbit (*to himself*) Silly little bird.

Sudden noises from a distance make Rabbit turn and listen eagerly. Heavy vehicles approaching. Headlamps swing across the stage momentarily dazzling Rabbit. The vehicles stop. Doors bang. Distant voices are heard

Music 4

Voice 1 Right lads. Cup of tea. Then unload.

Voice 2 OK. Brew up, Charlie.

Voice 3 Righto.

Voice 4 (*singing*) Charlie put the kettle on . . .

Laughter. Rabbit listens transfixed

Rabbit (*to himself*) Big Ones.

He scuttles to his burrow and disappears

The noises of the Big Ones recede

Squirrel descends the tree

Squirrel Make it snappy, Rabbit. I can't afford to dilly dally, shilly shally, mystery or no mystery. (*He notices Rabbit is not there*) Rabbit? Rabbit. (*He goes to the burrow entrance. Calling*) Rabbit? (*Louder*) Rabbit? (*He gives up and calls up the tree*) Dunnock!

Pause

Dunnock!

Dunnock appears through the foliage

Dunnock Dear oh dear oh dear. What is it, Squirrel?

Squirrel Play a little game with me, would you?

Dunnock I beg your pardon?

Squirrel Play a little game with me, would you?

Dunnock Sorry, Squirrel, too busy. Didn't know you liked games. Ask Rabbit to play with you.

Squirrel No!

Dunnock He likes games.

Squirrel No, you bird of little brain. I mean, is this your idea of a joke?

Dunnock Joke?

Squirrel Leading me on a wild rabbit chase.

Dunnock Sorry, you've lost me.

Squirrel I've lost Rabbit.

Dunnock Him too? Dear oh dear. Where is he?

Squirrel If I knew that, I wouldn't be saying I'd lost him. He's not here. You really are very thick, Dunnock.

Dunnock There's no call for rudeness. Rabbit wanted to see you about some mystery.

Squirrel The mystery is, where's Rabbit?

Dunnock Search me, Squirrel.

She disappears

Squirrel tries the burrow again

Squirrel (*calling*) Rabbit!

No reply. Squirrel goes to leave. He spies an acorn

Ah!

Music 5

(*Picking it up*) At least it's not a totally wasted journey. (*He goes to climb the tree, and suddenly sees the white cross. He reacts mystified, then, like Rabbit earlier, stretches up to feel it. He, too, gets paint on his paw. Bemused, he climbs back up the tree, carrying his acorn. As he climbs*) Out of my way, Dunnock.

Squirrel disappears

Dunnock (*off*) Charming. (*Calling after him*) It's not my fault he's not there.

Dunnock reappears through the foliage and climbs down the trunk

(*to herself*) Hope he's all right. It's not like him to be unreliable. He did seem in a bit of a state, though. (*She goes to the burrow and calls down it*) Rabbit? Rabbit! Are you there? I took your message. Rabbit!

Rabbit enters from off-stage—from the direction in which the Big Ones' voices came from. He is breathless and agitated

(*Still looking down the burrow*) Rabbit!

Rabbit What are you doing?

Dunnock (*turning*) Looking for Rabbit. (*Turning back and calling down the burrow*) Rabbit!

Rabbit Yes?

Dunnock What? Oh it's you! Silly me. Where did you spring from?

Rabbit My back door. Over there. Where's Squirrel?

Dunnock He's been and gone.
Rabbit Been and gone?
Dunnock Arrived and departed.
Rabbit But I haven't spoken to him yet.
Dunnock That's on account of the fact you weren't here when he arrived.
He arrived after you departed. *You* arrived after *he* departed. A matter of
bad timing, if you ask me.
Rabbit I'm not asking you, Dunnock, I'm telling you, to get Squirrel down
here. Now.
Dunnock Again?
Rabbit Quickly, please. It's serious.
Dunnock It *is*. I'll never get my jobs done at this rate.
Rabbit Go!
Dunnock Oh, all right.
Rabbit Hurry!
Dunnock (*climbing the tree*) Dear oh dear oh dear oh dear . . .

Dunnock disappears

As Rabbit watches her depart, the noises of the Big Ones return. Rabbit freezes

Music 6

Voice 1 Right, lads, the party's over. We got a job to do.
Voice 2 OK. Unload the gear.
Voice 1 Shift yourself, Charlie!

Laughter

Rabbit reacts frightened and scampers down his burrow

*As he does to, the Lights fade. The noise of heavy mechanical gear being
unloaded, and an engine being turned on, fills the air and increases in intensity
as the scene change takes place. The base of the tree disappears (flown or
revolved) and the main set, half-way up the tree is revealed*

*It incorporates several levels, dominated by, at stage level, the "hollow"—the
home of Owl. This should include a closed-off section, which could be like a
hut, complete with door; however, it might be more appropriate, and less
fantasy-orientated, to have a section partitioned off by a leafy equivalent of a
bead curtain. Owl's hollow becomes the dominant acting area, in which
meetings of the tree community take place. Other important locations are a
hole in the trunk, in which Squirrel has his drey, an upper level, partly covered
with foliage, where Mistlethrush has her nest, and a branch the other side from
which Bat can "hang". The actor playing Bat should appear to be upside down,
with his head on his arms. Branches should provide walkways between these
locations, perhaps using scaffolding and steps disguised with leaves and ivy*

*As the noises of the Big Ones' working recede, Lighting reveals Dunnock
climbing towards Squirrel's drey. She carries cleaning implements—brush
(made from twigs) and dusters (made from leaves). The brush could be
strapped on her back. She whistles as she climbs*

As Dunnock reaches Squirrel's drey, we hear his voice from inside

Squirrel (*inside*) Twenty-three, twenty-four, twenty-five ...
Dunnock Excuse me. Squirrel.
Squirrel (*inside*) Twenty-five, twenty-six ...
Dunnock (*louder*) Squirrel!
Squirrel What is it? I'm busy. Twenty ...
Dunnock It's Rabbit.
Squirrel (*popping out, carrying acorns, or perhaps an improvised abacus*) Rabbit? Where?
Dunnock Down there.
Squirrel Down where?
Dunnock Down there. Waiting.
Squirrel Oh not again. Where was I? Twenty-five? Twenty-six? I've lost count now. I'll have to start all over again.
Dunnock Sorry, Squirrel.
Squirrel *You're* sorry? My annual acorn tally's important, Dunnock. I don't do it for fun. Winter has a nasty habit of creeping up on us. I must be prepared. It's serious.
Dunnock I know Squirrel. But Rabbit's serious too. I've never seen him so serious.
Squirrel Oh, very well. But this is the last time. Up, down, up, down.
Dunnock Life's full of them, they say.
Squirrel What?
Dunnock Ups and downs. Shall I clean out your drey while you're gone?
Squirrel Yes, please, Dunnock. But don't interfere with my acorns, please. They're all sorted.
Dunnock Right. Mind how you go.

Squirrel climbs down, round the trunk and out of sight

Squirrel (*as he goes*) Dilly dally, shilly shally ...

   Squirrel disappears

Dunnock starts sweeping the entrance to the drey. Suddenly, from above her, comes a strident, shrill, out-of-tune singing, the sort of singing that human beings might practise in the bath. It is Mistlethrush

Music 7

Mistlethrush   La la la la laaaah!
                   La la la la laaaah!

A bundle of nesting material falls from above on or near Dunnock. She reacts irritated, and sweeps it up

> Spring, spring
> Makes me sing
> My happy tuneful song.

More nesting material descends on Dunnock

Dunnock What's going on up there? (*She clears up the nesting material*)
Mistlethrush   La la la la laaaah!
                    La la la la laaaah!

More nesting material falls

Dunnock (*calling*) Hey! Up there, whoever you are.

Foliage parts, revealing Mistlethrush in the throes of making her nest. She untidily builds it around her in a slap-dash manner. She leans out

Mistlethrush 'Allo, dearie.
Dunnock Oh it's you, Mistlethrush. Morning.
Mistlethrush Nice one! (*She sets to work on her nest again, slapping on grass and twigs and odd shreds of Polythene bag material. She sings even more stridently*)

> Spring, spring
> Makes me sing
> 'Cos summer won't be long!

More nesting material gets flung out on to and around Dunnock, who gamely tries to collect it

Dunnock Mistlethrush, must you be so messy?
Mistlethrush Sorry, dearie, I'm building my nest.
Dunnock I can see that. (*Holding up the fallen nesting material she has collected*) I thought you were building it down here for a moment.
Mistlethrush Sorry, dearie. Just getting sorted out. Be a love and bring me those bits back.
Dunnock (*resigned*) On my way. (*She climbs up to Mistlethrush's nest*)
Mistlethrush Got some lovely bits of plasticy stuff this year. Big Ones leave it behind after their picnics. Very good stuff for insulting, that, my fella says.
Dunnock Insulting?
Mistlethrush Yeah, insulting, infiltrating, something like that.
Dunnock Insulating.
Mistlethrush Exactly! Keeps the eggs warm. And the babies when they hatch. (*Receiving the nesting material from Dunnock*) Ta, dearie. You're a treasure. (*She starts building again, making a terrible mess*) Now, this bit here, that bit there. Whoops! Lost that bit.
Dunnock Do you want a bit of help?
Mistlethrush Oh, would you? I'm not much good at it, am I? Funny, I'm not what you'd call domesticized . . .
Dunnock Domesticated.
Mistlethrush Exactly. But come springtime I get this feeling, all warm and cosy and material . . .
Dunnock Maternal.
Mistlethrush Exactly. And I fling myself into a flavour of activity getting ready for the big day. Oo I can't wait. What about you dearie? Are you laying this year?

Dunnock In a few weeks, I expect.

She works away. Mistlethrush does very little

Mistlethrush Lovely. Listen, I've written this pretty little lullaby for my babies. I'll teach it to you. Might come in useful. (*She sings, loudly and off-key*)

Music 8

> Hush your beak
> Close your eyes
> Go to sleep
> And rest all the rest of you
> Mum is tired
> Don't squawk or squeak
> Hush your beak.

Dunnock has listened with a pained, patient expression

Good, innit? That'll nod 'em off in no time.
Dunnock I think it might keep them awake!
Mistlethrush Eh?
Dunnock It's excruciating.
Mistlethrush Exactly. Knew you'd like it. (*Looking at her nest*) Oo, you are getting on a treat. A palace! Ta, dearie, everso. (*She starts to sing again — a dreadful din*)

> Spring, spring——

Dunnock (*interrupting*) I'd, er, better be off. Squirrel's drey to muck out. (*She starts to leave*)
Mistlethrush Bye, dearie!

Music 9

(*Singing*)   Spring, spring
             Makes me sing
             My happy tuneful song.

She works away on her nest again as Dunnock descends and enters Squirrel's drey. More nesting material falls down

> Spring, spring
> Makes me sing
> 'Cos summer won't be looooooong!

Suddenly Jay arrives — on the branch below, near Squirrel's drey. He is brashly confident, and carries a kind of "suitcase" for his wares

Jay What music fills my ears?
Mistlethrush (*looking down*) Who's that?
Jay Such tone. Such pitch. Such artistry.
Mistlethrush Ooh! You flashy flatterer.
Jay Jay's the name, madam. Travelling salesbird supreme.

Mistlethrush I know you! Long time no see.

Jay I have been on a flight of exploration, madam, spreading my wings far and wide in search of marketable merchandise. Scouring the countryside for new and exciting lines to offer my lucky customers at bargain prices. What do you fancy?

Mistlethrush Nothing, dearie. I'm too busy building my nest.

Jay Aha! See my selection, perfect for the use of. (*He opens his coat. Inside his wares are neatly displayed*) Dried grasses, bracken, quality mosses, badger hair, sheep's wool for extra warmth, polythene and paper. Pick your own, mix 'n' match, yours for the modest sum of two acorns. Can't say fairer than that.

Mistlethrush Not today, thank you, Jay.

Jay Do me a favour.

Mistlethrush I've got all I need, dearie. I'm almost ready to lay.

Jay Aha! Think ahead, madam. Think of when your eggs hatch. Think of all those hungry little beaks to feed. No problem. (*He opens the other side of his coat, revealing more merchandise*) I've got crab apples, juicy slugs, calorie-stuffed caterpillars, mouthwatering worms, specially selected spiders, meaty maggots and crunchy moths. Take your pick.

Mistlethrush Sorry, dearie, come back next week.

Jay Your loss, dear lady, not mine. Happy laying.

Mistlethrush Tata, Jay.

She disappears into her nest, dropping more nesting material by Jay. He eagerly picks it up, then drops it

Jay Ugh. Most inferior. (*He thinks again*) Might sell it second-hand. (*He approaches Squirrel's drey*) Wakey, wakey! Anyone at home?

Dunnock appears, carrying rubbish from the drey

Dunnock Not today, thank you, Jay.

Jay Give a bird a chance, Dunnock! Where's Squirrel?

Dunnock Out. I'm doing his cleaning.

Jay Aha! Glad you said that. Ideal for the use of. (*He opens his suitcase, displaying more wares*) Look at this little lot. Bark scourer, lichen loosener, fungus flusher, mildew stripper, leafmould remover. Tried and tested. Satisfaction guaranteed.

Dunnock No thanks.

Jay I'm only asking one acorn per item.

Dunnock I've got no acorns. Squirrel's your best bet for acorns. He's got stacks of them in there.

Jay Really?

Dunnock Nightmare it is trying to clean round them, believe you me.

Jay (*apparently sympathetic*) I'm sure, I'm sure.

Dunnock Now, if you'll excuse me, I must get rid of Squirrel's rubbish. (*She sees Mistlethrush's nesting material*) Oh, no. (*To herself*) Mistlethrush, I've just cleaned this branch. Dear oh dear oh dear.

Music 10

*She passes Jay and starts clearing up. She doesn't notice Jay take the
opportunity to enter Squirrel's drey. He checks no-one is looking, then darts
inside, returning almost immediately carrying two acorns. Dunnock finishes
clearing and turns round. Jay hastily hides the acorns*

You still here?

Jay Er ... thought I'd wait for Squirrel. Any idea when he'll be back?

Dunnock Anybody's guess. I must get on, anyway. Owl's hollow to muck
out yet. See you.

Jay Good day, dear lady.

*Dunnock sets off for Owl's hollow. When she arrives, she disappears inside the
inner sanctum*

*Jay stows away the two acorns in his suitcase or in his pockets. He checks the
coast is clear and pops back inside Squirrel's drey*

*Suddenly Squirrel appears, scrambling up from behind the tree. He is
breathless and agitated*

Squirrel (*calling*) Owl! Owl!

*He goes towards Owl's hollow, as Jay emerges from the drey with two more
acorns. Squirrel doesn't see Jay, who nervously pops back in the drey*

Owl!

Dunnock appears from Owl's inner sanctum

(*Shouting*) Where's Owl?

Dunnock Owl's out.

Squirrel She would be.

Dunnock See Rabbit?

Squirrel Yes, yes. Where is she?

Dunnock Still hunting, I dare say.

Squirrel Never around when she's needed.

Dunnock Don't blame me, Squirrel. I only work here.

Squirrel I know Dunnock. I'm sorry, but it's urgent.

*Jay sees his chance. He hurries out with two acorns, grabs his things and hides
behind the trunk, unseen by Squirrel*

Dunnock It's always urgent.

Squirrel (*shouting*) It's *very* urgent.

Mistlethrush (*leaning out of her nest*) Excuse me. Could I ask you to lower
your voices?

Squirrel Don't you start, Mistlethrush.

Mistlethrush That's just it dearie. I *have* started. My eggs are coming and I
have to conserve.

Dunnock Concentrate.

Mistlethrush Exactly. So, please. A bit of hush for Mistlethrush. (*She
disappears*)

Squirrel (*in a loud whisper*) Dunnock! Please. Let me know the moment Owl
gets back.

Dunnock Right. (*She goes back into Owl's inner sanctum*)
Squirrel (*muttering as he returns to his drey*) What a day! What a day! (*He enters his drey*) What a—(*With a shriek*) What on earth? (*He darts out again. Calling*) Dunnock! Dunnock!

Mistlethrush leans out of her nest

Mistlethrush Hush, please!
Squirrel Sorry, Mistlethrush.

Mistlethrush flounces out of sight

(*Calling*) Dunnock!

Dunnock emerges from Owl's inner sanctum as Squirrel arrives

Dunnock Not again. I told you. Owl's out.
Squirrel I know, I know, you silly little bird. Listen, I thought I asked you not to interfere with my acorns.
Dunnock You did and I didn't. Devil of a job I had cleaning round them.
Squirrel They're not all there.
Dunnock *You're* not all there, if you ask me. Been funny all morning.

Jay creeps back from behind the tree, and enters Squirrel's drey again

Squirrel Come with me. I'll show you. (*He drags Dunnock towards his drey*) Come on.
Dunnock Oh dear, oh dear. Calm down, Squirrel.
Squirrel I'm perfectly calm. I——

He is cut short by the sight of Jay emerging from the drey, carrying another two acorns.

Thief! Thief!
Jay Ah! No! I can explain.
Squirrel Caught in the act!
Jay No, no. Listen, Squirrel. I er ... I lost my way.
Squirrel Lost your way? I've lost my acorns. You've stolen them!
Jay No, no, no. These are *my* acorns.
Squirrel Your acorns?
Jay Yes. I was hoping to sell them to you. You're one of my best customers.
Squirrel Liar!
Jay Squirrel, please! My reputation!
Squirrel Clear off!
Jay You're making a big mistake!
Squirrel Clear off!

Dunnock looks on philosophically as Mistlethrush looks down from her nest

Mistlethrush (*shrill*) Will you shut up!

The others freeze in surprise

Have a little consternation.
Dunnock Consideration.

Mistlethrush Exactly.

Squirrel Sorry, Mistlethrush. Serious business down here.

Mistlethrush It's not exactly a barrel of laughs up here! Laying eggs is a very painful progress.

Dunnock Process.

Mistlethrush Exactly. And you can shut up too, cleverdick Dunnock. Ooh! (*A cry of pain as her labour pains force her back into the nest*)

Dunnock I'd better go and help her.

Dunnock climbs up to Mistlethrush. Both remain hidden behind the foliage

Squirrel (*to Jay*) You see the havoc you cause?

Jay Havoc? Have a heart, Squirrel. Just a bit of honest trading.

Squirrel Honest? You stand there holding my acorns and call it honest?

Jay Yes. Well. Perhaps I overstepped the mark. Call it quits, eh? (*He hands the acorns back to Squirrel*)

Squirrel Call it what you like. Just flap your wings and fly away. (*He throws an acorn at Jay*)

Jay All right. All right. Keep calm.

Squirrel I'm perfectly calm! (*He throws another acorn*)

Jay Ow! You've made your point!

Squirrel quickly gets more ammunition from inside the drey, and throws it

Squirrel Scarper!

Jay Ow!

Squirrel Now!

(*NB: In the original production, to really throw the acorns proved impractical: Squirrel mimed throwing in threatening fashion, and Jay reacted*)

He has forced Jay back towards Owl's hollow

Suddenly they are both frozen by the appearance of Owl from her inner sanctum

Owl Enough!

Both Squirrel and Jay react nervously

Squirrel Sorry, Owl.

Jay No harm meant.

Owl I will not suffer brawling. This is a civilized tree.

Squirrel Yes, Owl.

Owl We are a civilized society.

Jay Yes, Owl.

Pause

Squirrel Good hunting, Owl?

Owl Disastrous. (*Threateningly*) I'm starving.

Squirrel Oh dear.

Jay May I be of service, Owl? (*He opens his coat*) Caterpillar? Slug? Very tasty.

Owl Unsubstantial. Junk food. Do you have a mouse?
Jay Er, no. But I could do you a vole.

Owl advances, as Jay starts to delve in his suitcase. Owl simply takes the suitcase, calmly turns and heads back to her hollow

Owl Thank you, Jay.
Jay That's four acorns, please.
Owl (*turning threateningly*) I beg your pardon?
Jay (*nervously*) Four acorns?
Owl No, thank you.
Jay I meant ...
Owl (*charmingly threatening*) But I'm sure Squirrel would appreciate four acorns.
Jay But Owl!
Owl Now.
Jay (*defeated*) Yes. Yes. My pleasure. Here you are, Squirrel. (*He hands over the acorns he stole earlier*) One, two, three, four.
Squirrel Thank you, Jay. How generous. Good day.
Owl Good day, Jay.

Jay mumbles and disappears behind the tree

Squirrel Thanks, Owl.
Owl I think justice prevailed.
Squirrel Yes, indeed. Er ... Owl, could I have an urgent word? You see ...
Owl Not now, Squirrel. Hunting makes me tired. Unsuccessful hunting makes me exhausted.
Squirrel Yes, but——

A sudden scream of pain from Mistlethrush's nest above

Mistlethrush Aaaaaagh!
Owl (*with a jump*) What on earth's that?
Squirrel Mistlethrush laying. It's a painful process.
Owl I know the feeling.

Dunnock leans from above, by the nest

Dunnock (*excited*) One egg laid. Number two coming! (*She sees Owl*) Morning, Owl. I've cleaned your hollow.
Owl Thank you, Dunnock.

Another shriek from Mistlethrush

Mistlethrush Aaaaaah!
Dunnock Excuse me. (*She disappears to help Mistlethrush*)
Owl (*yawning*) See you later, Squirrel. (*She turns to go*)
Squirrel But, please, Owl, it's important. Let me——
Owl Later, Squirrel, later.
Squirrel But *please*, you see, Rabbit——

Another sudden interruption. Loud singing:

Music 11

Bat (*from behind the tree*)
>   You gotta keep
>   Hanging on
>   Baby
>   Gotta keep
>   Hanging on ...

Owl Oh no, Bat's back!

Bat enters, heavily "into" the rock song playing (unheard by us) through his large headphones. A "Walkman"-style battery pack is attached to his belt

Bat   You gotta keep
>   Hanging on
>   Baby
>   Gotta keep
>   Hanging on ...

As though in a trance, he jigs up and down, making loud percussion-type noises in accompaniment to the music

>   Shubba dubba boom boom
>   Shubba dubba wow!

Owl He's in one of his trances again. Wake him up.

Squirrel goes to Bat and waves frantically at him. Dunnock peers down to see what all the noise is about

Squirrel Bat! Bat!
Bat   Be-dum dum dum dum
>   Pow!

He nearly knocks Squirrel over

>   You gotta keep
>   Hanging on——

In desperation Squirrel pulls the plug out of the battery pack. Bat immediately stops dancing

Hey, Squirrel, baby, you turned me off. I was all turned on and in the groove. In the groove and on the move. Pow! Pow! Pow! My, what a night! (*He sees Owl*) Hi, Owl, baby!

Owl Don't baby me, Bat. Where have you been? You stink.

Bat I've been raving, Owl baby. Down the Battery Disco Tree. Where all the best bats hang out. The joint was jumping and I was flying!

Owl He's high as a kite. Go to your perch and sleep it off. Help him, Squirrel.

Bat I'd far sooner swing in your cosy little hollow, Owl baby.

He tries to reach it, but Squirrel leads him away to his perch

Owl You come near my cosy little hollow and I'll swallow you for breakfast.

Bat OK, Owl, baby. Don't get uptight, right? (*He tries to perch upside down*) Let it all hang out, like little old me.

He keeps losing his balance. Squirrel tries to help him. He sings jerkily

> You gotta keep . . .
> Hanging on . . .
> Baby . . .
> Gotta keep . . .
> Hanging . . . on . . .

He finally balances and starts snoring. Squirrel returns to Owl

Owl Did I say this was a civilized tree? A civilized society? Sometimes I wonder.

Squirrel *I* wonder, Owl, if you could please listen . . .

Owl I've told you, Squirrel.

Squirrel ⎫   But it's vital that you listen. Rabbit has news. *The Big*
             ⎬ (*together*) Ones . . .
Owl   ⎭   I want some rest. Now go away and leave me alone—

Music 12

Owl The Big Ones? (*She pays attention immediately*)

Squirrel Yes.

Owl What? Where?

Squirrel I don't know, but Rabbit says please come.

Owl Why didn't you tell me before?

Squirrel I tried, Owl, I did try.

Owl (*preparing to leave*) I'll meet you down there. I don't like flying so low in broad daylight, but it's a risk I'll have to take.

She disappears round the trunk, preparing to fly down

Squirrel Thank you, Owl.

Squirrel hastens to climb down the tree. He disappears

Music 13

Jay emerges from hiding. He checks the coast is clear, laughs softly, retrieves his suitcase from Owl's hollow, then enters Squirrel's drey

Bat wakes and looks at Owl's hollow

Bat (*delighted*) Owl's out! Groovy! (*He goes down to it and settles upside down, enjoying the comfort*)

Suddenly a shriek from above—Mistlethrush

Mistlethrush Aaaaaah!

Bat loses his balance and topples. Jay pops his head out of the drey in alarm. Dunnock leans out over Mistlethrush's nest

Dunnock Two!

Black-out

Music 14

As the scene changes back to the base of the tree, we hear the grating mechanical sound of a digger. The sounds continue as the Lights come up on the base of the tree

Squirrel is descending. He goes to Rabbit's burrow

Squirrel (*calling*) Rabbit! Owl's coming! Rabbit!

Owl arrives, as though she has just landed

Owl (*tense*) Where is he?
Squirrel He'll be here. Look, Owl. The mystery. (*He shows Owl the white cross*) What does it mean?
Owl I wish I knew, Squirrel. (*Suddenly*) What's that noise?

The digger noise increases. Owl and Squirrel listen intently. Then, distant voices

Voice 1 Another one over here, Tom.
Voice 2 OK (*Calling*) Charlie. More earth. Get a move on.
Voice 3 Coming.
Owl Rabbit was right. Big Ones.

Suddenly Rabbit emerges from his burrow, caked with earth and terrified

Rabbit (*breathless and almost hysterical*) No! No! Please! No!
Squirrel Rabbit, Owl's here.
Rabbit Owl, Owl. Tell me I'm dreaming. Tell me it's not true. It can't be true! Help me! Help me!
Owl Pull yourself together, Rabbit. What's happened?
Rabbit I tried. I did try. There was nothing I could do. Murderers! Murderers!
Owl Rabbit! Tell us. Calmly.
Rabbit Big Ones. Filling in the burrow. Earth pouring down. Friends and relatives struggling, suffocating. Buried alive. (*He breaks down, sobbing, and collapses into Squirrel's arms*)
Squirrel He's fainted. Oh Owl, what are we going to do?
Owl Back up the tree, quick.
Squirrel What about Rabbit?
Owl Him too.
Squirrel Up there? But how, Owl, how?
Owl Like before.
Squirrel Before?
Owl (*taking hold of Rabbit*) Before you were born, Squirrel. One winter it rained for days. The waters rose and flooded out Rabbit's burrow. I lifted Rabbit and his friends and relatives to safety in the tree till it was over. Emergency rescue. Like this one.

Music 15

The noise of the digger and earth pouring into the burrow interrupt. Owl and Squirrel react

See you at the hollow. And Squirrel.
Squirrel Yes, Owl?
Owl Get Dunnock to call a crisis meeting!

Squirrel starts to climb. Owl prepares for take-off, grasping Rabbit firmly

The Lighting fades and the scene changes back to half-way up the tree. Meanwhile, noises increase and become more menacing. Regular beat of the generator. Then voices

Voice 1 Ready for the main action, Tom?
Voice 2 Ready, boss.
Voice 1 Got enough cable?
Voice 2 Reckon so.
Voice 3 Where do we start, boss?
Voice 1 Small ones first. Work up to the big one, eh?
Voice 3 Right.

Laughter

The Lights fade up. Bat is snoring, asleep in Owl's hollow. Jay is stuffing acorns into his suitcase. Suddenly, Mistlethrush bursts into song

Music 16

Mistlethrush (*hidden*)
            La la la la laaaaah!

Jay and Bat react

  (*Appearing, jubilant*)
            La la la la laaaaah!
            Spring, spring
            Makes me sing
            A celebration song.

Jay (*wincing*) Wish I had your headphones, Bat!

But Bat is asleep again

Mistlethrush   Spring, spring
            My eggs are laid
            And they'll hatch before too long.

  Dunnock appears by the nest

Dunnock Congratulations, Mistlethrush. Four eggs!
Mistlethrush Ta, dearie. And thanks for all your help.
Dunnock Fancy a bite to eat?
Jay (*who has been listening*) How's about some fresh mistletoe berries, Mistlethrush?

Mistlethrush Oo, my favourites. How much?

Jay No charge, Mistlethrush. My present to congratulate you on a safe delivery.

Mistlethrush Oo, ta. (*Imitating him*) Can't say fairer than that!

Dunnock I'll get them for you.

She starts to go down to Jay, who finds the berries

Squirrel scampers up to the hollow

Squirrel Right. Action stations, everyone!

Music 17

Dunnock You still at it, Squirrel? Up, down, up, down.

Squirrel Dunnock, Owl says you're to call a meeting.

Dunnock A meeting? Why?

Squirrel You'll find out. It's an emergency.

Dunnock Oh dear. Right. Come on everybody. Meeting. (*She goes to Bat*) Wake up, you smelly Bat. (*Lifting one of his earphones*) Wake up! Meeting.

Bat overbalances

Bat OK, OK. Stay cool, Dunnock.

Squirrel (*to Jay*) You still here?

Jay Just on my way.

Squirrel You'd better stay. (*Calling up*) Mistlethrush!

Dunnock She's just laid her eggs.

Squirrel Can't help that. (*Calling*) Mistlethrush! Down here.

Mistlethrush (*leaning out*) Don't be daft, dearie. Can't leave my eggs.

Squirrel Owl's orders.

Mistlethrush But——

Squirrel Emergency.

Dunnock Cover the eggs up. Keep them warm.

Jay (*seeing the seriousness of the situation*) Take her all this stuff. That'll help. (*He opens his coat, revealing the nesting material*)

Dunnock Thank you, Jay.

She takes the nesting material and hurries up to Mistlethrush. During the next section we see both birds carefully covering the eggs in the nest

Squirrel (*to Bat, who has gone back to sleep*) Bat!

Bat I'm up! I'm up!

Owl and Rabbit enter round the trunk to the hollow. Rabbit is conscious but weak. He crumples into the hollow, watched by the others

Owl Everybody here?

Squirrel Mistlethrush and Dunnock on their way.

Owl Now, you all know Rabbit.

Bat He looks rougher than I feel.

Owl He's in a bad way, I'm afraid.

Jay Here. Try this. (*He produces a sprig from his suitcase, and puts it under Rabbit's nose*) Garlic mustard. Sniff this, Rabbit.

Rabbit sniffs, then sneezes violently. He recovers somewhat

Dunnock and Mistlethrush arrive in the hollow

Mistlethrush What is all this? If my eggs don't hatch, Owl, there'll be trouble.
Owl Hush, Mistlethrush.

Mistlethrush sees Rabbit

Mistlethrush What's that Rabbit doing here?
Owl Hush! Rabbit, can you hear me?
Rabbit (*nodding*) Where am I?
Owl Safe. Up the tree. Among friends. Now tell us all what happened. Calmly.
Rabbit Noises. Big Ones. Voices. Machines. Went to look. Met my friends and relatives other side of the field.
Squirrel What did you see?
Owl Quiet, Squirrel. Take your time, Rabbit.
Rabbit Big machines.

Music 18

Sharp metal. With pointed teeth. Wire. Then one machine clears Big Ones' rubbish. I thought, "Good. Rubbish dangerous." But then . . . then . . .
Owl (*gently*) Yes?
Rabbit Another machine digs earth . . . and comes towards us. Panic. Fear. Down burrow. Then earth pouring down on us. Run through burrow. Scrabble to survive. Many friends and relatives can't make it. Buried alive . . . (*He breaks down*)

A shocked pause

Mistlethrush But why?
Owl Who can fully understand the Big Ones? Not us.
Jay Butchers.
Bat You stick with us, Rabbit, baby. You'll be OK.
Dunnock You're safe up here.
Rabbit No. White cross.

Music 19

Squirrel Yes! Tell them about the white cross.
Rabbit On the tree. Paint. Still wet.
Owl I saw it too.
Mistlethrush What does it mean?
Rabbit Others. Other white crosses. On the other trees. Danger! Danger!
Owl All right, Rabbit, relax. (*To the others*) We must find out more. Bat, how's your radar?

Bat A1, Owl. Shall I tune in? See what I can suss?
Owl Please.

Bat goes to his perch and "tunes in". A sudden noise interrupts

Cuckoo (*from behind the tree*) Yoo-hoo! Yoo-hoo! Yoo-hoo!

Cuckoo enters. She is loud and colourful and very tanned. She carries a travelling bag

> Well, hi there, fans, I'm here to say
> I've just flown in on my holiday
> From Africa is many a mile
> So now I'm here I'll stay awhile
> Yoo-hoo!

Mistlethrush springs up

Dunnock Oh dear, oh dear. It's Cuckoo.
Mistlethrush (*fury rising*) This is the last straw!
Cuckoo Mistlethrush! Yoo-hoo!
Mistlethrush (*rushing to her nest*) Get rid of her! Get rid of her!
Cuckoo Aren't you glad to see me? I sure am glad to see you!
Mistlethrush I bet you are.
Owl Cuckoo. You've chosen a bad time. You're welcome, but——
Mistlethrush (*leaning from her nest*) Welcome? She's about as welcome as a bolt of lightning.
Cuckoo That's not nice.
Mistlethrush And you think what you did to me was nice? Last year? You sly bird. You dumped your egg in my nest, scarpered back off to the sun, and left me to bring up your brat.
Cuckoo And a fine job you made of it. Then he flew right back to his momma in Africa.
Mistlethrush And that's what you can do. Fly right back to Africa. Now!

All try to placate Mistlethrush. Suddenly a loud noise interrupts and freezes everyone into silence. The savage, harsh grating noise of a chainsaw

Music 20

Squirrel Shhhhhh!

All look, horrified. After ten seconds or so, the sound of a falling tree

Owl Bat?
Bat (*tuned in to his radar*) No echo! I'm getting no echo!
Owl Explain.
Bat The tree the other side of the field. (*Realizing*) The Battery Disco Tree. Like it's gone. Disappeared.

The noise of the chainsaw returns and increases to an almost painful level as the characters look at each other in fear and the Lighting fades to Black-out

The noise of the chainsaw suddenly cuts out

Curtain

ACT II

As the House Lights fade, the screech of the chainsaw is heard. It rises in intensity

Music 21

Then the sound of another tree falling. Nearer than the earlier one

The Lights come up on on the hollow. All except Mistlethrush are gathered as at a meeting, with Owl "in the chair". Rabbit is recuperating. Mistlethrush is in her nest, visible. All listen, horrified

Squirrel How many's that?

Bat Five trees down. And they're getting nearer.

Owl Bat, how many trees before they reach ours?

Bat Two. Three. Depends on which direction they take.

Cuckoo I don't see what all the fuss is about. We're quite safe here, aren't we?

Squirrel Don't be stupid, Cuckoo. The Big Ones are clearing the land, the trees. *Our* tree, maybe.

Mistlethrush Anyway, it's all right for her. She doesn't live here. This is our home, Cuckoo.

Dunnock We'll have to move.

Squirrel Why should we move? Mistlethrush is right. This is our home. It's always been our home.

Owl There must be something we can do.

Rabbit The white cross.

Music 22

Owl What about it?

Rabbit The Big Ones painted white crosses on lots of trees. Why?

Jay As a sign, if you ask me. To remind them which ones to remove, so to speak.

Owl That means they wouldn't cut down our tree ...

Bat ... if it didn't have a white cross on it! Yeah yeah!

Owl Exactly. Dunnock, could you clean it off?

Dunnock I could try.

Jay Take my samples, Dunnock. Only the best. No rubbish. Clean off anything with that lot. (*He gives her his suitcase*)

Dunnock Thanks, Jay.

Jay All part of the service.

Rabbit Let me help. I'm better now, Owl. Take me down. I can do a bit of scouting too.

Owl Good idea ...

Sudden interruption—nearer

Voice 1 OK, Charlie. Turn on.

The noise of the chainsaw. All freeze

Music 23

Owl Bat!
Bat (*tuning in*) After this one, we're next in line.
Owl Quick! Before it's too late.

Owl, Rabbit and Dunnock (grabbing cleaning things) go behind the trunk, preparing to fly down, as the Lighting fades and the chainsaw noise increases

Then, in the Black-out ...

Voice 3 Here she goes!

Crashing noise of a tree falling

The scene changes back to the base of the tree

Dunnock and Rabbit are scrubbing out the cross. Already much of it has gone. Jay's suitcase lies open

Voice 1 OK, lads, chain her up.

Noises of chains being attached to the next-door tree. Dunnock and Rabbit scrub furiously. Dunnock tires

Dunnock Oh dear, oh dear.
Owl (*whispering*) Keep going, Dunnock. Here, let me. (*She desperately joins in*)
Voice 1 Right, lads, take her away.

The noise of a heavy vehicle dragging the tree away

Next one, Charlie.

Heavy footsteps of two men approach. There is one area of white paint still visible, near the bottom of the trunk

Dunnock I can't do it, Owl. This bit's dried solid. I can't ...
Owl Too late! Retreat!

Owl and Dunnock escape behind the tree, remembering to take Jay's suitcase. Rabbit starts to go, then, realizing white paint is still visible, flings himself against it, hiding it. He lies motionless

The footsteps stop

Voice 3 Funny. Where's the cross?
Voice 1 Let's have a bit more light on the subject.

A sudden flash of light illuminates the trunk, moving up, down and across

Nothing.
Voice 3 This one staying, then, boss?
Voice 1 Must be, Charlie.

The light finds Rabbit

What's that?
Voice 3 Rabbit. Dead by the look of it.
Voice 1 Died of fright, I dare say.

Laughter

Fancy a rabbit stew for your supper, Charlie?
Voice 3 No, no!
Voice 1 I'll get it for you.

Footsteps, plus shadows in the torchlight

Suddenly, from behind the tree, Owl hoots, menacingly

Stone the crows, what's that?

Owl hoots again

Voice 3 An owl, I reckon, boss.
Voice 1 Don't like owls. Spooky creatures. Come on. We'll do the next one.
Voice 3 Right.

The light and footsteps recede, as the Big Ones go

Owl and Dunnock hurry round to see Rabbit

Dunnock Well done, Rabbit! You really fooled them.
Owl Congratulations, Rabbit. That was very brave.
Rabbit Thanks, Owl. Your hoot really got 'em going ...

Footsteps returning

Music 24

Look out, they're coming back!

Owl and Dunnock dash behind the tree. Rabbit throws himself against the remains of the cross and feigns dead

Voice 3 (*calling*) It's over here somewhere!
Voice 2 (*from a distance*) Trust Charlie to leave the saw behind!
Voice 1 (*from a distance*) ha, ha.
Voice 3 I'll give you a sore behind in a minute! Here it is. Sorry, boss.

The footsteps recede. Pause

Rabbit gets up and looks tentatively off. Then ...

Rabbit (*in a loud whisper*) All clear!

Owl and Dunnock emerge

Owl Thanks again, Rabbit.

Rabbit A bit close that was, Owl.

Dunnock I'd better finish scrubbing off this paint. (*She starts work again*)

Owl Good idea, Dunnock. Can't be too careful. Then we'd better go back up. Report to the others. A celebration is called for. You come too, Rabbit.

Rabbit I don't think I'd better ...

Owl You must. You are the hero of the hour. Thanks to you, our home is safe. We are safe.

Rabbit Well, it's very kind of you, Owl, but I'd rather not. I think I'd better see what's left of the burrow.

Owl Of course. Very selfish of me. Your friends and relatives haven't been as lucky as us.

Rabbit (*quietly*) No.

Dunnock Finished!

Owl Excellent. Up we go, then, Dunnock.

Dunnock 'Bye, Rabbit. Thanks again.

Rabbit 'Bye, Dunnock. 'Bye, Owl.

Owl Goodbye, Rabbit.

Rabbit starts to go

And Rabbit!

Rabbit stops

Rabbit Yes, Owl?

Owl I hope you find at least some of your friends and relatives safe. I really do.

Rabbit Thanks, Owl.

Rabbit goes

Music 25

The noise of the chainsaw attacking the next tree makes Owl and Dunnock get moving

They disappear, preparing to fly back up the tree, as ...

The Lighting fades and the noise intensifies

The scene changes back to half-way up the tree. The noise continues as the Lights come up

Bat, Jay, Cuckoo and Squirrel wait tensely in the hollow. Mistlethrush looks down anxiously from her nest

A tree is heard to fall. All react, nervous and powerless

Cuckoo I don't understand your Big Ones. Why do they cut down your trees?

Mistlethrush What's it matter to you, Cuckoo? You're only here a couple of weeks a year.

Cuckoo It matters much. In Africa there are so few trees. They say Big Ones die because of this. Here they have trees. Why do they cut them down?

Squirrel The Big Ones move in mysterious ways, Cuckoo. Who are we to reason why?

Bat Cut the homespun philosophy, Squirrel, baby. I've got a sounding on the airwaves.

All attend

(*Tuned in*) Gotta work this out. The tree that's just fallen was west, right?

He points. The others agree

The one that fell before was east, right?

He points in the opposite direction. The others agree

Then, my, my, I think we've done it. The Big Ones have missed our tree out. Yippee!

Relief and general cheers

Jay Snack, anyone? (*He takes food from inside his hat or pockets and offers it round*) Caterpillar, slug? First-class festive fare.

They accept gratefully

Squirrel I have to admit I misjudged you, Jay. I'm sorry. You've been very helpful.

Jay That's big of you, Squirrel. I appreciate that. Fancy an acorn? (*He gives him one*)

Squirrel Thank you.

Jay It's one of yours anyway.

Squirrel goes to react, but thinks better of it and smiles. All laugh

Cuckoo Come on down, Mistlethrush! It's party time!

Mistlethrush Thanks, dearie, I'd love to, but I can't leave my eggs.

Cuckoo I'll egg-sit for you. Very good egg-sitter I am.

Mistlethrush Oh, would you? I could do with a stretch ... (*realizing*) ... hang on, not blooming likely! Don't you come anywhere near my nest, Cuckoo. I know your game. Get up here, get rid of one of my eggs, lay one of your own and leave me to do the dirty work. Egg-sitter indeed!

Cuckoo Only trying to help.

Mistlethrush Ha!

Bat (*suddenly tuning in*) Hey, hey! Cool it, you chicks. Something on the line.

All attend

(*Eventually*) It's OK. It's Owl.

Owl and Dunnock enter from behind the trunk

Owl Emergency over! Celebration!

All cheer

Squirrel What happened, Owl? Did you manage to clean off the white cross?

Owl Well, yes . . .
Jay Jay's classy cleaning products up to scratch, eh?
Owl Yes, thank you, Jay. But it was Rabbit who truly saved the day.
Dunnock We hadn't finished scrubbing off the paint, so Rabbit covered it
  up by pretending to be dead. And the Big Ones couldn't see it!
Squirrel Good for Rabbit! Hip, hip, hip . . .
All Hooray.
Bat On with the party!

Music 26

Come, on, Owl baby, let's let it all hang out! *He starts gyrating.*

Owl (*looking shocked, then melting*) Why not? Go, Bat, go! Groovy, groovy!

*Bat sings. The others pick up the song and dance with wild enthusiasm.
Mistlethrush jogs about above*

Bat	You gotta keep hanging on
All	Baby, gotta keep hanging on
	You gotta keep hanging on
	Baby, gotta keep hanging on.
	You gotta keep hanging on
	Baby, gotta keep hanging on
	You gotta keep hanging on
	Baby, gotta . . .

*Suddenly noises of the Big Ones make all freeze. First a loud whistle—a
piercing human whistle to attract attention*

Music 27

Then . . .

Voice 1 Oy! Charlie! Shift yourself.

Running footsteps. Breathless arrival of Charlie

Voice 3 What is it, boss?
Voice 1 Look here.

Rustle of paper

I thought there was something fishy going on.
Voice 3 What do you mean?
Voice 1 Of course this tree has to come down. It's on the plan, see? Clear as
  daylight. No question.
Voice 3 Then why no white cross?
Voice 1 Don't ask me? Administrative error. Who cares?
Voice 3 What do we do, then, boss?
Voice 1 Don't be stupid, Charlie. It's marked on the plan so down it comes.
Voice 3 Right, boss.
Voice 1 Now, it's the biggest of the lot, right? I want the chainsaw, the most
  powerful one we've got, with the yellow cable. And we'll need the
  generator. Tell Tom.

Voice 3 Right, boss.
Voice 1 And get a move on. We don't want to be here all night.

Footsteps recede

A shocked hush on the tree. Eventually . . .

Squirrel That's it then.

Pause

Owl We should have known. We can never beat the Big Ones.
Jay Evacuate. Leave the tree. That's the answer. The only answer.
Cuckoo You could all come home with me. To Africa.
Mistlethrush I don't want to go to bloomin' Africa. This is my home.
Squirrel I agree, Mistlethrush. If my home is to die, I will die with it.
Mistlethrush Well. I didn't say *that*, dearie.
Dunnock Forgive me, Squirrel, but that's a silly attitude. Dear oh dear, we
  can't just give up! (*She is embarrassed by her own vehemence*)
Bat (*urgently*) Turn down the volume, Dunnock, I'm picking up . . . hey,
  that's crazy!
Owl What?
Bat Cloud. Low cloud. Very low.
Owl Cloud?
Squirrel (*sniffing the air*) What's that smell?

All sniff the air. Suddenly smoke begins to appear

Jay That's not cloud, Bat. It's smoke!

Dunnock and Cuckoo begin to cough. Sound of burning wood

Owl They're burning the cut-down trees. (*She coughs*) We've no choice
  now. We'll suffocate if we stay. Everybody leave. Abandon tree!

The noise of flames increases. A red glow is seen to one side. More smoke

  Meet down the bottom!

Signs of panic as the creatures dash about

Mistlethrush (*screaming*) No. No. My eggs. My eggs. I won't leave my eggs!
Dunnock Bring them with you!
Mistlethrush I can't!
Cuckoo You can, Mistlethrush! Let me help.
Mistlethrush You?
Cuckoo Please!

All are affected by the smoke, which becomes thicker

Squirrel (*who has rushed to his drey*) What about my acorns?
Owl You'll have to leave them.
Squirrel But we'll starve! And I've been storing them for days.
Jay Take them with us, Squirrel. Drop them down the tree! Bat, give us a
  hand!

Music 28

Squirrel passes out acorns to Jay, who passes them to Bat, who throws them down the tree. Meanwhile, Mistlethrush hands down two eggs to Cuckoo, or even drops them down. Or maybe Dunnock works a relay system up and down. Two eggs go in Cuckoo's bag, packed with nesting material that Mistlethrush flings down. Dunnock takes Jay's "suitcase" for the other two eggs. In the confusion, perhaps an egg is mistakenly thrown to Bat as an acorn—then carefully passed back down to Cuckoo and Dunnock. In the midst of this hive of activity, Bat freezes

Bat (*tuning in*) Big Ones returning! Big Ones returning!
Owl Hurry! Hurry!

Noises of vehicles, burning logs, and chainsaws intensify as the Lighting fades on the scene of urgent activity

The scene changes back to the base of the tree

As the Light fades up, there is still smoke, but not as much

> *The evacuees arrive. Squirrel climbs down the tree. Owl, Dunnock, Mistlethrush, Bat, Cuckoo and Jay come round the trunk, having flown down. Bat uses his radar to check for safety. Cuckoo and Mistlethrush immediately improvise a nest in the root formations, checking that the eggs are well wrapped. Dunnock helps*

All here? Mistlethrush?
Mistlethrush Here.
Owl Jay?
Jay Here.
Owl Bat?
Bat Here.
Owl Cuckoo?
Cuckoo Here.
Owl Dunnock?
Dunnock (*returning Jay's "suitcase" to him*) Here.
Owl Squirrel?
Squirrel Here.
Owl Any sign of Rabbit?
Squirrel No, Owl. Shall I go and look for him?
Owl No. We stick together. Wait for Rabbit. He knows the field better than us.

They huddle together

Jay Anyone hungry?
All (*muttering*) No, thank you, Jay.

Mistlethrush perches on her improvised nest. Dunnock and Cuckoo fuss round her

Mistlethrush I think the eggs are OK. Ta everso, Dunnock. (*To Cuckoo*) And you, dearie.

Cuckoo Quiet, Mistlethrush. Try to rest.

Mistlethrush No, I'm very grateful. And if we come through all this, Cuckoo, feel free to dump your rotten egg on me as usual.

Cuckoo Thank you.

Bat (*tuned in*) Owl! (*After a pause*) Rabbit.

Rabbit enters, breathless

All listen eagerly

Owl Well?.

Rabbit (*not defeated*) The field's a right old mess, Owl. They've filled in the burrow. Killed all my friends and relatives. They're burning the trees. Chaos it is, chaos.

Bat (*tuned in*) Big Ones approaching.

Music 29

The rumble of a heavy vehicle approaching

Owl We'd better move on.

Rabbit No. There's nowhere to move on to. And this is the last tree. We can't let it die like the others.

Squirrel Hear, hear!

Owl But we can't stop the Big Ones.

Rabbit Maybe not. But we can show a bit of resistance. Stand up for our home.

Jay Go down fighting, eh?

Bat Right on!

Mistlethrush We can't fight them.

Dunnock But we can't desert our home.

Rabbit Good for you, Dunnock. What do you say, Owl?

The heavy vehicle stops. Doors slam. As voices are heard approaching, Owl makes her decision. Standing centre, she stretches out her hands. The others, as if mesmerized, join her. They defiantly, bravely, form a chain in front of the tree

Voice 2 Right, boss. Let's get it down. Charlie, how are you doing?

Voice 3 Nearly ready.

The sound of machinery being unloaded

Voice 2 Big one, this. What do we do, boss? Start up top?

Voice 1 I reckon.

Voice 2 Polish this one off, be home in time for tea, eh?

Laughter. Suddenly a yellow cable swings into view

Voice 3 Chainsaw ready, boss.

Voice 1 Electrics ready?

Voice 2 Ready!

Voice 1 OK, Charlie. Turn on.

The ghastly noise of the chain-saw. Reflections from the savage metal glint on the faces of the tree folk. Suddenly, accompanied, as it were, by the noise of the chain-saw, they sing, loudly and defiantly

Music 30

Tree Folk   Save our tree
                     Don't let it fall
                     Save our tree
                     Save us all.

                     Save its trunk
                     And leafy dome
                     Save our tree
                     Save our home.

                     Can't you see
                     This tree
                     Has a history
                     Its own traditions
                     And laws
                     Can't you see
                     This tree
                     Is a community
                     A world as alive
                     As yours.

                     Save our tree
                     Please set it free
                     Save our tree
                     Let it be.

                     This tree's ours
                     But it's your tree too
                     Share it, care for it
                     The way we do.

                     Save our tree
                     Don't let it fall
                     Save our tree
                     Save us all.

The singing stops

Voice 2 What's all this then?
Voice 1 Some sort of demo?

Laughter

Music 31

Clear off, the lot of you. Vermin, that's what you are. Dirty, stinking vermin. Go on, Charlie, do your worst.

The noise of the chainsaw increases. Suddenly Owl leaps forward as though to attack. She is followed by Jay and Cuckoo. But in vain. They mime being beaten back. Mistlethrush screams. The noise of the chainsaw attacking wood. The cable swings. The tree folk look upwards. A branch crashes down from above. The tree folk huddle against the trunk

(Optional: More branches crash down, hopefully identifiable—Bat's "perch", part of Owl's hollow, Mistlethrush's nest.)

Light increases to suggest that the chainsaw is coming lower. The wretched tree folk cower and maybe scream, clinging on to each other for dear life

Suddenly Rabbit breaks out. As though in a trance of defiance. He moves to the cable, grabs it and bites it

Music 32

A flash. The fuse has blown. The noise of the chainsaw cuts out

Rabbit shudders with the force of the electricity, then crumples in a heap. The others look on aghast. Squirrel approaches Rabbit, puts his ear to Rabbit's heart, then turns to the others and shakes his head. Rabbit is dead

Music 33

The tree folk sadly hum the tune of their "Save Our Tree" song, backing away, holding hands. The Lighting narrows to a pin-spot on Rabbit. The others melt into the back ground

Rabbit stirs, gets up and begins to take off the rabbit parts of his costume. He becomes Mr Bunn again

Mr Bunn Will Mistlethrush's eggs ever hatch? Will Cuckoo lay her egg in Mistlethrush's nest and fly back to Africa? Will Bat find another Battery Disco? Will Owl, Dunnock and Squirrel ever lead a normal life again? Will Jay find other trees on which to carry out his business? Who knows? It's all in the imagination, anyway. Just a story. Who cares? Well, I care. And perhaps it *could* happen. It *will* happen if Mr Jay and Mr Batty have their way, if they do as they want and clear Turner's Field for their children's playground.

Mr Bunn has wandered to the side of the stage, still in his pin-spot, as the scene is changed back to the public platform in the village hall

The other characters return to take their places as at the beginning of the play—Mrs Wise, Mrs Dunnock, Mr Storer, Mr Jay, Mr Batty, Mrs Cook and Mrs Thrush

So, I put it to the meeting. What right have we to kill the See-Saw Tree, a tree that has lived longer than any of us? It would take three minutes, with a chainsaw, to destroy the work of three hundred years. And jeopardize the lives of all its inhabitants. Animals, birds, insects. And for what? So that Mr Batty and Mr Jay can line their pockets with the pocket money of our children.

The Lighting comes up on the meeting, and in the auditorium

Mr Jay Madam Chairman, I object to that. We are providing a much-needed amenity in this area, and all this sentimental twaddle is totally irrelevant.

Mr Batty Hear, hear.

Mrs Thrush Hear, hear. We want that playground.

Mrs Cook I agree. You can't stop the wheels of change. It's called progress.

Mrs Wise Thank you. Well, we've heard the arguments. Earlier your votes suggested a children's playground was a good idea. But, please, let's vote again, this time on whether Mr Jay and Mr Batty should be allowed to cut down the See-Saw Tree. Please raise your hands if you want it cut down.

Mrs Dunnock counts hands. They include Mr Jay, Mr Batty, Mrs Thrush and Mrs Cook, Mrs Dunnock gives the number "for"

Mrs Wise Now please raise your hands if you do *not* want the See-Saw Tree cut down.

Hopefully the audience unanimously raise their hands. Mrs Dunnock starts to count

The result, I think, can be said to be unanimous, The See-Saw Tree must stay.

Mr Bunn and others lead applause. (For alternative endings to suit any eventuality on the voting, see page 36)

Mr Jay Now hang on a minute. Earlier on you said you wanted the children's playground. Now you say you want the See-Saw Tree. You can't have it both ways.

Mr Storer I think, if I may be allowed to speak, Madam Chairman, we *can*.

Mrs Wise Go ahead, Mr Storer.

Mr Storer Of course Mr Jay should have his children's playground—it's an excellent idea. But why can't the See-Saw Tree be part of it? For the children, indeed for all of us, to see and enjoy.

Mrs Dunnock And why shouldn't Mr Batty provide a plank and give the tree a see-saw, as in the old days. Then today's children can play on it.

Mrs Wise Well, Mr Batty?

Mr Batty Ah. Well, it's not as simple as that. All the plans'll have to be redrawn. That costs money.

Mr Jay I think it's fair enough, Batty. You've still got your video games and fruit machines, and they've got their tree.

Mr Batty Well ... I suppose ... it's quite a neat idea ... (*Visualizing a sign over the entrance to the playground*) "The See-Saw Tree Children's Playground" ... it's good! Yes! OK, I agree!

Applause, led by Mr Bunn

Mrs Wise Good. Thank you all for coming. I declare the meeting closed. And I suggest a celebration. To celebrate the saving of ...

Mr Bunn The rebirth of ...

All THE SEE-SAW TREE!

All happily sing and dance, encouraging the audience to join in each chorus

Music 34

Song: The See-Saw Tree

An actor accompanies the song on guitar or piano (the piano could be part of the village hall set)

All

Sing the story of
The See-Saw Tree
Standing proud and free
Such a sight to see.
May we always share
With the creatures living there
The story of
The glory of
The See-Saw Tree.

The verses could be sung by all in unison, or solo lines could be allocated if required

All (*or solos*)

A long time ago a squirrel found
An acorn and buried it in the ground
Came the rain and the sun
On the fertile earth
And the story had begun
With an oak tree's birth.

Using a song-sheet, the actors encourage the audience to join in the chorus

All (+ *audience*)

So
Sing the story of
The See-Saw Tree
Standing proud and free
Such a sight to see.
May we always share
With the creatures living there
The story of
The glory of
The See-Saw Tree.

All (*or solos*)

As the seasons changed and the years went by
The oak tree flourished and soared up high
So its trunk and its branches
And its roots could give
The animals and birds
A place to live.

All (+ *audience*)

So
Sing the story of
The See-Saw Tree

Standing proud and free
Such a sight to see.
May we always share
With the creatures living there
The story of
The glory of
The See-Saw Tree.

All (*or solos*)   The tree looked down on the old high street
The local landmark, the place to meet.
And ev'ry May Day
It set the scene
For the singing and the dancing
On the village green.

All (*+ audience*)   So
Sing the story of
The See-Saw Tree
Standing proud and free
Such a sight to see.
May we always share
With the creatures living there
The story of
The glory of
The See-Saw Tree.

All (*or solos*)   A tree with a future, witness of the past
Steadfast and stable in a world changing fast
Let the sun shine down
Let the see-saw sway
Long live our tree
As the children play.

All (*+ audience*)   So
Sing the story of
The See-Saw Tree
Standing proud and free
Such a sight to see.
May we always share
With the creatures living there
The story of
The glory of
The See-Saw Tree.

May we always share
With the creatures living there
The story of the glory of
The glory of the story of
The story of the glory of
The See-Saw Tree.

*The characters freeze at the end of the song. We hear the creak of a see-saw.
The Lights slowly fade*

CURTAIN

ALTERNATIVE ENDINGS

Endings to suit (hopefully) any eventuality

Each ending starts from Mrs Wise's invitation to vote *against* the cutting down of the tree.

1. If the vast majority of the audience vote *against*:

Mrs Wise The result is virtually unanimous. The See-Saw Tree must stay. (*Etc. as before*)

2. If the audience are divided, but clearly more are against than *for*:

Mrs Wise The majority are against. So the See-Saw Tree must stay. (*Etc. as before*)

3. If voting looks even:

Mrs Wise We are divided. No clear majority.
Mr Storer If I may be allowed to speak, Madam Chairman.
Mrs Wise Go ahead, Mr Storer.
Mr Storer We may be divided on whether or not to cut down the See-Saw Tree, but we all agree a children's playground is a good idea. Now, why can't the See-Saw Tree be part of the Children's Playground?
Mrs Dunnock And why shouldn't Mr Batty ... (*Etc. as before*)

4. If all the audience vote *for* cutting down the tree (hopefully unlikely):

Mrs Wise Well, the meeting clearly decides to cut down the See-Saw Tree. Mr Jay, Mr Batty—you have your go-ahead.

Mr Jay and Mr Batty shake hands, delighted

Thank you all for coming to the meeting. Good day.

All collect their papers and leave

(NB: The play would therefore finish without *the song)*

FURNITURE AND PROPERTY LIST

ACT I

The Village Hall

On stage: Table *On it:* small bell, notepad, pencil
 Chairs

Off stage: Broom **(Mrs Dunnock)**
 Maps, pictures **(Mr Jay)**
 Diagram **(Mr Batty)**
 Rabbit's costume **(Actor)**

The Bottom of the Oak Tree

On stage: Base of oak tree with root formations. *On trunk:* large white painted cross
 Entrance to Rabbit's burrow
 Ivy climbing tree, concealing scaffolding or ladder rungs
 Foliage above
 Grass, acorns on ground

Further up the Oak Tree

On stage: Middle section of tree trunk, including, at various levels:
 Owl's hollow with closed-off section and door or leafy curtain
 Squirrel's Drey. *In it:* acorns, rubbish
 Mistlethrush's nest. *In it:* nesting material
 Bat's branch
 Branches as walkways between the above, with leaves and ivy to disguise
 scaffolding or steps

Off stage: Brush, dusters **(Dunnock)**
 Suitcase containing wares, including cleaning materials **(Jay)**

Personal: **Jay:** merchandise including nesting material and food on inside of coat
 Bat: headphones and personal stereo

The Bottom of the Oak Tree

On stage: As before

Personal: **Rabbit:** mud caked on body

Further up the Oak Tree

On stage: As before

Check: Mistletoe berries, sprig of garlic mustard in Jay's suitcase

Off stage: Travelling bag **(Cuckoo)**

ACT II

Further up the Oak Tree

On stage: As before

The Bottom of the Oak Tree

On stage: As before, plus:
Jay's suitcase and cleaning materials
Most of white cross removed

Further up the Oak Tree

On stage: As before, plus:
4 eggs in Mistlethrush's nest

The Bottom of the Oak Tree

On stage: As before

Off stage: Bag with nesting material and 2 eggs **(Cuckoo)**
Suitcase with nesting material and 2 eggs **(Dunnock)**
Yellow cable **(Stage Management)**
Branch crashing down from above **(Stage Management)**
More branches **(Stage Management)**—optional

The Village Hall

On stage: As before

Off stage: Song-sheet **(Actors)**

LIGHTING PLOT

Property fittings required: nil

1 interior, 2 exteriors

ACT I

To open: House lights up, general lighting on stage

Cue 1	**Mr Bunn:** "The See-Saw Tree." *Spot on* **Mr Bunn;** *fade other lighting on stage and house lights down*	(Page 3)
Cue 2	**Mr Bunn** (*echo effect*): "Just imagine, just imagine . . ." *Fade spot on* **Mr Bunn;** *bring up dawn lighting on base of oak tree*	(Page 3)
Cue 3	As sound of heavy vehicles approaching is heard *Headlamps swing across stage*	(Page 4)
Cue 4	As **Rabbit** scampers down his burrow *Fade lights*	(Page 6)
Cue 5	When ready *Bring up general morning lighting*	(Page 6)
Cue 6	**Dunnock:** "Two!" *Black-out*	(Page 17)
Cue 7	When ready *Bring up lighting on base of tree*	(Page 17)
Cue 8	**Owl** prepares for take-off, grasping **Rabbit** firmly *Fade lights*	(Page 18)
Cue 9	When ready *Bring up general lighting on tree*	(Page 18)
Cue 10	Characters look at each other in fear *Fade to black-out*	(Page 21)

ACT II

To open: Black-out

Cue 11	After sound of tree falling *Bring up lighting on tree*	(Page 22)
Cue 12	**Owl, Rabbit** and **Dunnock** go behind trunk *Fade to black-out*	(Page 23)
Cue 13	When ready *Bring up lighting on base of tree*	(Page 23)

Cue 14	**Voice 1:** ". . . a bit more light on the subject." *Flash of light illuminates trunk, moving up, down and across*	(Page 23)
Cue 15	**Voice 1:** "Must be, Charlie." *Light finds* **Rabbit**	(Page 24)
Cue 16	**Voice 1:** "I'll get it for you." *Shadows in torchlight*	(Page 24)
Cue 17	**Voice 3:** "Right." *Light recedes*	(Page 24)
Cue 18	**Owl** and **Dunnock** disappear, preparing to fly back up tree *Fade lighting*	(Page 25)
Cue 19	When ready *Bring up lighting on tree*	(Page 25)
Cue 20	**Owl:** "Abandon tree!" *Red glow to one side*	(Page 28)
Cue 21	As noises of vehicles, burning logs and chainsaws intensify *Fade lighting*	(Page 29)
Cue 22	When ready *Bring up lighting on base of tree*	(Page 29)
Cue 23	Noise of chainsaw *Reflections from metal glint on faces of animals*	(Page 32)
Cue 24	Branch crashes down; animals huddle against trunk *Increase light to suggest chainsaw is coming lower*	(Page 32)
Cue 25	Animals hum and back away, holding hands *Narrow lighting to follow pin-spot on* **Rabbit**	(Page 32)
Cue 26	**Mr Bunn:** ". . . pocket money of our children." *Fade pin-spot; bring up general lighting on stage and house lights up*	(Page 32)
Cue 27	Characters freeze at end of song; creak of see-saw *Slowly fade lights*	(Page 36)

EFFECTS PLOT

ACT I

Cue 1   **Mr Bunn:** "Just imagine."   (Page 3)
Echo effect on his voice

Cue 2   **Mr Bunn** becomes **Rabbit; Music 3**   (Page 3)
Chorus of birdsong

Cue 3   **Rabbit** (*to himself*): "Silly little bird."   (Page 4)
Sudden noises from a distance—heavy vehicles approaching, stopping, doors slamming, then distant voices of Big Ones as script page 4

Cue 4   **Rabbit** disappears   (Page 4)
Fade noises of Big Ones

Cue 5   As **Rabbit** watches **Dunnock** depart   (Page 6)
Voices of Big Ones as script page 6

Cue 6   **Rabbit** scampers down burrow; lights fade   (Page 6)
Noise of heavy mechanical gear being unloaded, engine turned on—increase in intensity as scene change takes place

Cue 7   When ready   (Page 6)
Fade Big Ones' noises

Cue 8   Black-out   (Page 17)
Grating mechanical sound of digger—continue

Cue 9   **Owl:** "What's that noise?"   (Page 17)
Increase digger noise; then fade digger and bring up distant voices of Big Ones as script page 17

Cue 10   **Owl:** "Like this one." Music 15   (Page 18)
Digger noise and sound of earth pouring into burrow

Cue 11   As lighting fades and scene changes   (Page 18)
Increase digger noise, more menacing, with regular beat of generator, then Big Ones' voices as script page 18

Cue 12   As lights fade up   (Page 18)
Fade digger and other noises

Cue 13   **Mistlethrush:** "Now!" All try to placate Mistlethrush   (Page 21)
Savage, harsh, grating noise of a chainsaw

Cue 14   **Squirrel:** 'Shhhhhh!" All look horrified   (Page 21)
Pause, then sound of falling tree

Cue 15   **Bat:** "Disappeared."   (Page 21)
            Chainsaw noise—increase to almost painful level

Cue 16   Lighting fades to black-out   (Page 21)
            Cut chainsaw noise suddenly

ACT II

Cue 17   As house lights fade   (Page 22)
            Screech of chainsaw, rising in intensity

Cue 18   After Music 21   (Page 22)
            Sound of tree falling, nearer than before

Cue 19   **Owl:** "Good idea ..."   (Page 23)
            Voice of Big One as script page 23, then noise of chainsaw—
            continue

Cue 20   **Owl, Rabbit** and **Dunnock** go behind trunk   (Page 23)
            Increase chainsaw noise; then voice of Big One as script page 23,
            followed by crash of tree falling

Cue 21   As lights come up on base of tree   (Page 23)
            Voice of Big One as script page 23; then noise of chains being
            attached to next-door tree

Cue 22   **Owl:** "Here, let me." (He desperately joins in)   (Page 23)
            Voice of Big One as script page 23; then noise of heavy vehicle
            dragging tree away; followed by heavy footsteps of 2 men
            approaching—continue

Cue 23   **Rabbit** lies motionless, hiding cross on tree   (Page 23)
            Footsteps stop; voices of Big Ones and effects as script pages 23–
            24

Cue 24   **Rabbit:** "... really got 'em going ..."   (Page 24)
            Footsteps returning

Cue 25   **Rabbit** feigns dead against cross on tree   (Page 24)
            Voices of Big Ones as pages 23–24; then footsteps, receding

Cue 26   **Rabbit** goes   (Page 25)
            Chainsaw noise, rising in intensity

Cue 27   Lights come up half-way up tree   (Page 25)
            Chainsaw stops; sound of trees falling

Cue 28   **All** (*singing*): "Baby, gotta ..."   (Page 27)
            Piercing human whistle, then voices and noises of Big Ones as
            pages 27–28

Cue 29   All sniff the air   (Page 28)
            Smoke appears, then sound of burning wood

Cue 30   **Owl:** "Abandon tree!"   (Page 28)
            Noise of flames increases; more smoke

Cue 31   **Cuckoo:** "Please!"   (Page 28)
            Increase smoke

Cue 32   **Owl:** 'Hurry! Hurry!"   (Page 29)
            Noises of vehicles, burning logs and chainsaws intensify

Cue 33   **Bat** (*tuned in*): "Big Ones approaching."   (Page 30)
            Rumble of heavy vehicle approaching

Cue 34   **Rabbit:** "What do you say, Owl?"   (Page 30)
            Heavy vehicle stops, doors slam, voices approach—voices and
            noises of Big Ones as script pages 30–31; noise of chainsaw

Cue 35   As animals stop singing   (Page 31)
            Voices of Big Ones as page 31; noise of chainsaw increases

Cue 36   **Mistlethrush** screams   (Page 32)
            Noise of chainsaw attacking wood; cable swings

Cue 37   **Rabbit** bites cable   (Page 32)
            Flash; cut chainsaw noise

Cue 38   Characters freeze at end of song   (Page 36)
            Creak of see-saw

MADE AND PRINTED IN GREAT BRITAIN BY
LATIMER TREND & COMPANY LTD PLYMOUTH

MADE IN ENGLAND